W9-CLX-813

Peanut Butter

BEFORE THE STORE

BY JAN BERNARD • ILLUSTRATED BY DAN McGEEHAN

Published by The Child's World®
1980 Lookout Drive • Mankato, MN 56003-1705
800-599-READ • www.childsworld.com

ACKNOWLEDGMENTS
The Child's World®: Mary Berendes, Publishing Director
The Design Lab: Design and production
Red Line Editorial: Editorial direction
Content Consultant: Kyle W. Stiegert, Professor and Director of Food System Research Group,
    University of Wisconsin-Madison

ISBN 9781609736798
LCCN 2011940076

PHOTO CREDITS
Tim Elliott/Dreamstime, cover, 1; James Lewis/Dreamstime, cover (inset), 1 (inset); Jiri Hera/Shutterstock
Images, 5; Danny E Hooks/Shutterstock Images, 7; Albert Lin/Shutterstock Images, 9, 30 (top); Shut-
terstock Images, 11; Wellford Tiller/Shutterstock Images, 13; Steyno & Stitch/Shutterstock Images, 21;
Debbi Smirnoff/iStockphoto, 24; Todd Media, Inc./iStockphoto, 29, 31 (top)

Design elements: Tim Elliott/Dreamstime

Printed in the United States of America

ABOUT THE AUTHOR

Jan Bernard has been an elementary teacher in both Ohio and in Georgia and has written curriculum for schools for more than seven years. She lives in West Jefferson, Ohio, with her husband, Tom, and their dog, Nigel. She has two sons who live in Columbus, Ohio.

Contents

CHAPTER ONE

Yummy Peanut Butter

How do you eat peanut butter? Do you like it on toast or on an apple slice? Peanut butter and jelly sandwiches are always a delicious choice. Some people eat peanut butter right out of the jar with a spoon. It is in candies, cookies, ice cream, and even brownies. Peanut butter is tasty and it is good for you, too. It is filled with protein that helps your body stay healthy. It also has a very good kind of fat that your body needs.

Have you ever wondered how peanut butter is made? There are many steps. The first step starts at a peanut farm. Peanuts cannot be grown everywhere. They need a long growing season. Places with long summers, such as Georgia, Alabama, and Florida, are best for peanut farms. And not just any peanut will do. Peanut farmers must use a certain kind of peanut to make the best tasting peanut butter.

Peanut butter is delicious and nutritious!

CHAPTER TWO

A Special Kind of Peanut

There are many different kinds of peanuts. Valencia peanuts are the sweetest kind. They are usually sold **roasted** or boiled. Spanish peanuts have the smallest **kernels**. They are used in candies and to make peanut oil. The best kind of peanut to use for peanut butter is the runner peanut. It works well because the nuts are all the same size. This helps them roast evenly. If the nuts were all different sizes, the peanuts would not roast as well. Some nuts would be burnt and others would not be roasted enough.

Peanuts are not actually nuts. They are related to **legumes**, such as peas! Also, peanuts go by other names. They include "groundnuts," "goobers," and "goober peas."

Runner peanuts make good peanut butter.

CHAPTER THREE

On the Peanut Farm

Farmers have two choices about where to get their peanut seeds. They can use seed that they saved from last year's crop. Or farmers can buy peanut seed from peanut seed dealers. Once farmers have their seed, they are ready to plant.

In April and May of each year, peanut farmers begin planting seed in the fields. The seeds are planted in long rows. The plants poke up through the soil in about ten days. Flowers bloom after 40 days.

Peanut plants are grown on a farm.

When the plant is fully grown, the peanut plant is about 18 inches (46 cm) tall.

Soon the flowers fall off. Then vines called **pegs** grow from the bottom half of the plant. The pegs dig into the ground. That is where the peanuts grow inside their shells. The peanuts will be ready to harvest four to five months after the seeds are planted.

In the fall, a tractor pulls a digging machine through the peanut fields. This machine pulls the plants out of the ground and breaks away their roots. Next a digger-shaker shakes the plants. It removes the dirt and turns the plants upside down. The plants are left to dry in the field for two or three days.

Peanuts grow in the ground.

When the peanuts have dried they are harvested with a **combine**. The combine picks up the plants, pulls the peanuts from the vines, and blows the peanuts into a hopper. A hopper is a container that is wide at the top and small at the bottom. The peanuts fall out of the hopper through a hole at its bottom. Finally the peanuts are put in a peanut wagon. In the peanut wagon the peanuts are dried even more with warm air. They are also inspected. The inspector looks at the size of the peanuts and makes sure they are safe to eat.

A combine is used to harvest peanuts.

CHAPTER FOUR

Shelling the Peanuts

Next the peanut wagons are sent to shelling plants. Shelling plants shell peanuts and different kinds of nuts, such as walnuts and almonds. At the shelling plant, the peanuts are cleaned. Stones, plant parts, and soil are removed. Then the peanuts move to the shelling machine. The shells are crushed off the peanuts. Next the peanut kernels and the shells pass through bursts of air in the machine. This separates the kernels from the shell parts. The kernels fall through a screen that sorts the peanuts by size.

Peanut shells are removed in a shelling machine.

What happens to all the peanut shells? They are not thrown away. Instead they are sold and used in other products. They include wallboard, kitty litter, and fireplace logs.

The peanuts move under a machine called an electric eye. It looks for any bad nuts or other things that should not be there and removes them. The peanuts are then bagged. Each bag weighs 100 pounds (45.4 kg).

Finally the peanuts can go to the peanut butter factory. They are shipped by truck or in railroad cars. Each railroad car can hold almost 200,000 pounds (91,000 kg) of peanuts. That's about the weight of 16 male elephants!

CHAPTER FIVE

A Peanut Butter Factory

Now the peanuts can become peanut butter. The first step is to roast the peanuts. The nuts move along a **conveyor belt** into a hot air roaster. Inside this machine, the peanuts are roasted at a high temperature. The roaster rocks gently. This helps the nuts roast evenly. The peanuts turn from white to golden brown. When they come out of the roaster, the nuts are very hot. They move into another machine. Inside the machine, the nuts cool quickly to room temperature. This machine has fans that pull the heat away from the peanuts. This stops the nuts from continuing to cook. It also keeps them from losing too much of their oil. If peanuts lose too much oil, they would make dry peanut butter. Most of the nuts move on to becoming peanut butter. But some nuts are pulled out. They are crushed later and added to jars that become crunchy peanut butter.

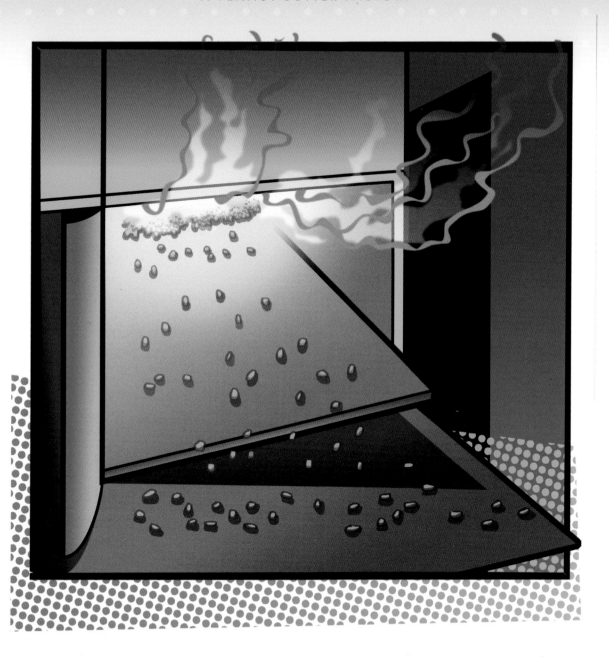

Peanuts move through a hot air roaster.

The next stop for the peanuts is the blancher. This large machine takes off the peanut skins. It rubs the nuts between two belts or brushes. The peanut is then split in two. Then the middle of the nut, called the heart, is taken out. The heart can be bitter. Then the nuts go through a machine that inspects them. This machine removes nuts that are scorched, rotten, or discolored.

Nothing is wasted in a peanut butter factory! The skins are sold to farmers for pig feed. The hearts are sold to companies that make bird food and peanut oil.

Peanuts are covered in a papery skin.

CHAPTER SIX

Grinding and Mixing

Next the peanuts start looking like peanut butter! In some factories, the nuts are dropped into a grinder by a person. In larger factories, nuts are fed into the grinding machine on a conveyor belt. The grinder is a very big machine with large blades that grind the nuts slowly. If the peanuts are ground too quickly, they heat up and start cooking again. Cold water may surround the grinding machine. It keeps the nuts cool. Sometimes the peanuts are ground twice. This makes the peanut butter extra smooth.

In most factories, the next step is to add salt, sugar, and **hydrogenated** vegetable oil. Without the hydrogenated oil, the peanut oil separates from the peanut butter. It ends up at the top of the jar. If the factory makes organic or natural peanut butter, it

Peanuts are ground into peanut butter in a grinder.

does not add hydrogenated oil. Sometimes the only ingredient in organic and natural peanut butter is peanuts!

If the peanut butter is going to be crunchy, chopped peanuts are added back. In some peanut butter factories, the peanut butter is **homogenized**. This is done in a machine. It uses high pressure on the peanut butter. It breaks up the fat in the peanut butter into small pieces. This makes the peanut butter really smooth and creamy.

Organic peanut butter is made without hydrogenated oil.

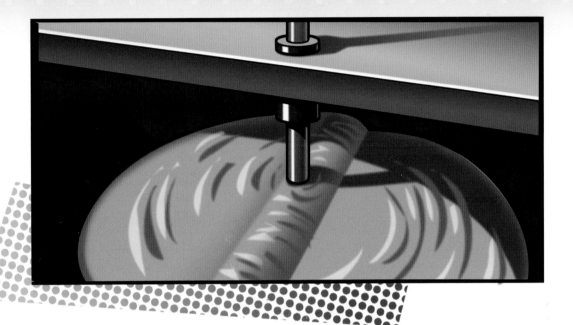

As the machines continue to mix the peanut butter, it gets very warm. To go into jars, the mixture needs to be cooled. The peanut butter is put into a refrigerated machine that looks like a very large rotating can. Inside, the peanut butter becomes cool enough to go into the jars.

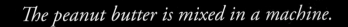

The peanut butter is mixed in a machine.

CHAPTER SEVEN

Into the Jars

Empty jars are put onto a conveyor belt. The jars pass under a large machine. The machine fills the jars with peanut butter. Then the jars are sealed. They move along to the capping machine. It screws caps onto the jars. The caps have a piece of **aluminum** in them called an aluminum seal. Next the jars are heated in another machine. The heat causes the aluminum seal to drop from the caps onto the jars. This forms a tight **vacuum** seal.

Finally a machine adds labels and stamps the date the peanut butter **expires** on the jars. The jars are then packed into shipping boxes. The peanut butter is now ready to be shipped to grocery stores.

Each jar is filled with the right amount of peanut butter.

CHAPTER EIGHT

Onto Your Sandwich

Peanut butter arrives at your local grocery store in large trucks. At the grocery store, there are many kinds of peanut butter to choose from. Some are on the shelves and some are in the refrigerated section. What kind of peanut butter will you choose? Do you like smooth and creamy or crunchy peanut butter?

Peanut butter makes a delicious lunch or snack. Try it on celery sticks. Or make some peanut butter cookies! But, a great way to eat peanut butter is in a sandwich. Don't forget the jelly!

Many kinds of peanut butter are at the grocery store.

PEANUT BUTTER MAP

1
PEANUT FARM

2
SHELLING PLANT

3
ROAST PEANUTS

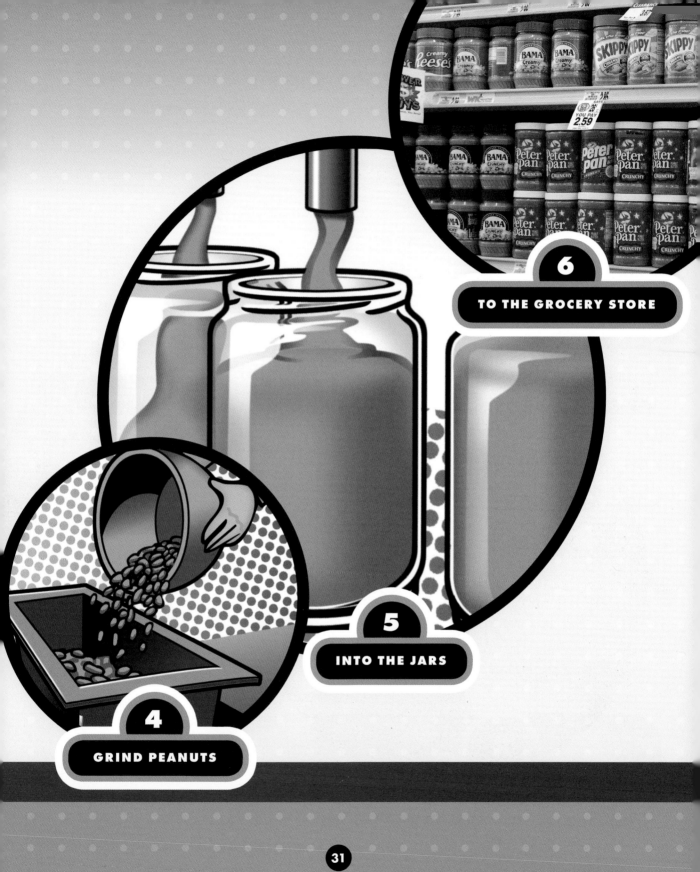

6 TO THE GROCERY STORE

5 INTO THE JARS

4 GRIND PEANUTS

31

aluminum (uh-LOO-mi-nuhm): Aluminum is a light metal with a silver color. Aluminum is used to seal peanut butter jars.

combine (KAHM-bine): A combine is a large machine used by farmers to gather and clean crops from a field. A peanut farmer uses a combine to harvest peanuts.

conveyor belt (kuhn-VAY-ur BELT): A conveyor belt is a moving belt that takes materials from one place to another in a factory. Peanuts move into machines on a conveyor belt.

expires (ek-SPIREZ): Something expires when it reaches the end of the time it can be used. You need to eat peanut butter before it expires.

homogenized (huh-MOJ-uh-nized): Food is homogenized when it is broken into small bits and spread evenly in the food. Some peanut butter is homogenized by a machine.

hydrogenated (hi-DRA-juh-nate-ed): A type of oil used in peanut butter. Hydrogenated oil is added to some types of peanut butter.

kernels (KUR-nuhlz): Kernels are the soft parts inside nuts' shells that are good to eat. Peanut kernels are taken out of their shells.

legumes (LEG-yoomz): Legumes are plants with seeds that grow in pods. Peanuts are legumes.

pegs (PEGS): Pegs are vines that grow from the bottom of a peanut plant into the ground. Peanuts grow from the pegs of a peanut plant.

roasted (ROHST-ed): Something is roasted when it is cooked in a hot oven. Peanuts are roasted before they become peanut butter.

vacuum (VAK-yuhm): A vacuum is a sealed space that has no gas or air inside. Peanut butter jars have vacuum seals on their caps.

BOOKS

Charlip, Remy. *Peanut Butter Party: Including the History, Uses, and Future of Peanut Butter.* Berkeley, CA: Tricycle Press, 2004.

Driscoll, Laura. *George Washington Carver: The Peanut Wizard.* New York: Grosset & Dunlap, 2003.

Micucci, Charles. *The Life and Times of the Peanut.* Boston, MA: Houghton Mifflin Harcourt, 2000.

INDEX

Visit our Web site for links about peanut butter production: childsworld.com/links

Note to Parents, Teachers, and Librarians: We routinely verify our Web links to make sure they are safe and active sites. So encourage your readers to check them out!